AFRICAN WRITERS SERIES
Editorial Adviser · Chinua Achebe

37
Satellites

AFRICAN WRITERS SERIES

Lenrie Peters

Satellites

HEINEMANN

LONDON · IBADAN · NAIROBI

Heinemann Educational Books Ltd
48 Charles Street, London W.1
PMB 5205, Ibadan · POB 25080, Nairobi
MELBOURNE   TORONTO   AUCKLAND
HONG KONG   SINGAPORE

SBN   435   90037-4

Printed in Malta by
St Paul's Press Ltd

Contents

To my parents

1

Skyflood of locusts
against the wind
trenches, excavations
mass scarecrow!

Cannonade of wings
in motion. Drilling
tongues of fire
macerate proportions

A bleeding earth
ferments in agony
success goes up in smoke,
returns a deluge of ruin

strike the heart
of life cold dead
surrender castrated hope
castrati voices of dust

muscles tighten
on mountain shoulders;
lynch the prophets!
verbiage of dust

A rope dangles
in red, clear
against other worlds
for all to see

Ecstasy and passion
have giant wings—
fly eternally through
tinsel world of things

Terror drives me,
grinds me corrupts me
to fornication and
myasthenic gravity of flesh

Heinous laughter
from the citadel
rings desert stench
in my soul

Locusts rotting
in the desert
rotting harshly
in the sun.

I am reminded
that scratching the
sky with bare nails
won't bring me heaven

Heaven is in
my blade of grass
my fire to survive
to cherish survival

Run me through
with odiousness, Politics
Isms, deceits, vanities
yet leave me the colour of truth

I will hold a light
to fight against the night
Come; come pilgrim through
winged canopy of locusts.

I should be ashamed
to hang up my
rags as I do
on the wall. What else?

I gasp with possibilities
only; I believe,
shout; I believe!
I BELIEVE.

2

Autumn burns me with
primaeval fire. Makes my skin
taut with expectation,
hurls me out of summer fatigue
on to a new Bridge of Sighs.

Somewhere I feel the heart
of the earth pumping, and down below
it bleeds in a million ripples.
I drop a sweet memory into
the flow and the cascading grips me with fascination

Great trees in transit fall
are made naked in langour of shame
solitary like actors on a stage
like stars, orphans, celebrities,
politicians, uncomfortably mysteriously like you and me.

But I will not mourn the sadness.
I will go dead-leaf gathering
for the fire in a slice of sunlight
to fill my lungs with odours of decay
and my eyes with mellowed rainbow colours

I will go creeping down tasselled
latticed tree-avenues of light
and listen to squirrel tantrums
punctuate the orchestration of autumn silence
and hold in my hand the coiling stuff of nature

4

Then I will love
Yes love; extravagantly under
the flutter of dying leaves
and in a shadow of mist
in wonder; for autumn is wonder and wonder is hope.

3

Sounds of the ocean
deep and bulging
with violent pattern
tumble in harmonies inside me
Sounds craving in action
for a glimpsed-at entity,
freedom from goodness.
The voice of God
grows soft and withers.
I remain armoury of values

Sounds of the ocean
trumpet, coil round
my hand in people's bellies
pools of blood
crawling segments with warmth
of bowel over my hand
Mistake is easy,

5

perhaps would free the conscience
like dropping a load of pregnancy
This life, an intolerable strain
another blemish on reality,
indelible stain must be saved.
The hand shakes
—a minor earthquake
in recreating a piece
of the world in darkness.
The margins approach
sweet conceit, bitter almonds
of extinction. The physical world
world of wood-chopping in winter
or incessant gazing into
Laparotomy wounds concatinate
in useful sanity with the
idea of good.
Sanity is lost as often
as breath is taken
but the adjustment is real
as pain, so we fall in love
with equilibrium.

Hand fumbling with bowel
or wringing out the brain
reaches no further than
the moment allows.
The good is undone
by deliberation of effect.

The good is like a star
shining out of a spider's
belly at night.

Curse the pursuit
and action; tranquillity
waits, the harvest reddens
hot with life. True colours
chime sweetly in the ear.
Seize the flesh of the moon
and hold it tight
in superlative enigma;
what are guts for?

Cycles of generations
centuries, wars, turn ever
a blade of grass or serpent
you, caught between spokes
selected for special agony
like the turbulence of flooding rivers
yields with magnificence of grace,
the good is always at the gate

Sounds of the ocean
bring all that is beyond
not within my grasp
a moving spirit, a destiny
a sense of largeness
groping in the dark

On hands and knees
mutilated by thorns
but groping still
from moment to moment
from earth to heaven
Thorns in the flesh
they say first nailed the Cross
we too must bear much
who rise to see the early frost

There will be wind and rain
I say the tumult of earth
will come again
There will be chaos and fumbling
of unconfident hands in bellies
and aches and pain
But there will be for each
who seeks with dedication
a solitary triumph of peace.

4

Wings my ancestors used
to fly from oppression, slavery
tincture of skin, arid birth and death
hang limp on my shoulders
with guilt of the oppressor.

I am a tamed eagle
no serpent in my claws.
They saw the world inviolate
created in seven days.
Amazedly I have inherited
the will to oppression
the love of it, the anger
staring out of darkness.
Today I give my blood for venison-victory
Tomorrow another's will wet the earth
libation to saints and freedom.
History cordially accepts it
as if ordained, but history is not inevitable.
Breezes from the past feather my curls
ancient animosities gnawing like giant bulldozers
compress my passage into a phallic stem
cycle of stagnation beginning at the end;
like science, exploding benefits
in a million worlds of chaos; computing eternity of
      chaos.
I would believe but I don't quite know what.
It would be easy to believe in something
quench the thirst, make it up with nature,
Chardin; like cosmic diplomats
comprising the cold-war of the soul. I would
      believe.
I see the stars adorned
immensity of chaos in space
revolutions of desire and object faced together.

9

I would say; the end of all things is eternal
and life makes living true.
Gilt-edged present invests the future,
rain and plant-growth intermingled
diadem of knowledge, profusion of time possibilities
shield my aching eyes from the sun
rub my sore gums with crystal salt.
I will go alone darkly till I have done.
Ignorant laughter, revenge
pass through me like memory
nibble my breath in gasps
then fall away like an outsize pair of pants.
Naked my conviction of doubt
primitive with Socrates and others
wandering bitterly alone, dying
wandering eternally in doubt.

There may be purer worlds to come
days crisp with settling snow and mushroom clouds,
mating in the park, leaves postured in protest,
world without conscience expiating guilt
protons whirling in energy
as befit a chain reaction.
That is the substance of things
the guidance is in me; in me.
But my blood is saturate of opium
smoking wastefully away
like the passion of summer days.

Sausage knees crawl in Alabama
Vietnam, Berlin; at the colour of my skin
religion, at the sound of contest
while voices rage with destruction;
I am a trustee for the future
before I have lived out today.
That is the substance of things
the guidance is in me.

5

Mine is the silent face
in the railway compartment
        in the queue
My flesh is drowsy with paint
        hideously faint
I travel through desperate
deserted places, my life
        ends in you vacantly
an empty tin rolling down
        catty cobbled alleys

I know the strength of the wind
in anger and the passion of waves
        —no floating mermaids—
Standing as I do
as all do

at the cutting chaotic edge of things
my youth burrows into the yearning
entrails of earth; dessicated.

A blank image stares out of flames
out of a dense affluent tomorrow
        studded with blame.
I tear at toasted locks of sunlight
reeds, parched reeds creaking in my lungs
It takes my life to hold the moon in focus.

Crushing dead glass in my strong hand
is worthless. Nothing bleeds, nothing relieves
it will not melt like snow
this emptiness, this hell I invented.

6

Watching someone die
is a fraudulent experience
The deep significance is felt
the meaning escapes
like a child's first punishment.
The dying ravish your strength
whether by throttle of convulsive gasp
or tideless fading away
like ancient familiar sounds in sea shells
the moment is the same

reinforced brutality to life
a rugged cliff bloodstained
with the agonising rhythm of many heads.
A cold demise; each
successive moment a banishment.
The terror is in leaving behind
the ache is in departing.

Humming fantasies crowd their stings
to seize and record the moment
the hands curl in spasm
to hold it back; this life, this infidel.
It is too late. Everything and nothing
has happened. A huge machine
the earth, grinds to a bolt-knocking halt.

It is the changing of the tide
at the boundary hour
Life like a handful of feathers
engulfed by cliff winds
one like yourself swept
Oh so swiftly into the anchorage of history
Tears and sighs; sighs and tears
stamping the leaden feet
the solid agony of years
they all abound.
One life or a million
contrived by nature or by man
greatly obscures the issue.

Face to face with dying
you are none-the-wiser
Yet it seems a most ignoble epitaph
'He was a man and had to die; after all.'

7

The fields are grey with corn
twilight colours in rhythm, music of time
cascading down centuries. Full disorder
of perishable flesh, order of values
nerve centre of Being in revolt.
Evening comes prematurely, unexpectedly
feet aching with years
broken by retreating clouds of sunshine
youth now past the Meridian
Clouds waving into and out of distance
beckon obscurely with limpid hints
tints on leaves, shades of feeling
majesty of knowing, perception.
Sudden hope glimmers in violets of undergrowth—
    deeply essential
all in a sense of passing time, of evening.

    Evening comes at last
    High noon seduced is laid.

The path lies steeply forward
crescendo of circles approaching darkness
circuitously direct like the heart
a metal spring perished in part
stringing limp years together.
The heart solid with remorse
(trifles, memories, lost affections)
stumbles in terror—tears of darkness
ask vain questions of the night.

Emotions in struggle
Fire-flies round the candle
knees bent in prayer
must also get up and go.
Mushroom voices like hollow
echoes in caves have their part.
It is the stuff of life
the non-acceptance
or laying down of arms;
burden of adventure
towards the unknown—
as we know it—richness of pursuit.
The road ends ever
where conflict is abandoned.

There were days of glory
before sunset; crucial with choices
alternatives seen wistfully—merried away—
figures dancing in the rain
against pillars of rain in moonlight

glancing passions and turmoil of brain
not so long ago.
Evening comes at last
Equilibriates the past.

8

Nobody knows
or cares where
Self comes from
or goes. My
knock slams
the door; reproaches
fall like soot

Another self
dives impenetrably
inwards trembling.
Blast of
autumn leaves
stuff the conscience
and ignite.

Self burns
totally alone.
The world is
singing, teeming
externally.

Massacre is
in my soul

Try to understand
even live pictures,
silent walls,
second class
Passports,
opportunities,
broken ankles.

Fill my
broken landscape
with tree clusters
thorns, the
rage of life;
decidedly
not bare

You cry
within me
claws screaming
flesh and blood
reaching for
sunlight
in darkness

multitudes
gather, deploy
like winter
shadows. Ears

cocked for
revenge shut
out sorrow.

I walk alone
in triumphant
irony of loneliness
a billion bones
round me rattle
with my cries;
all consumed

9

I want to
drag you out
shake your eyes
open with pictures
sounds and words
compel your imagination

Drag you to
your knees till
you sniff the
throwback of
my vision
with ease

thrill you
with sunsets
mornings; lies
behind the truth
with infinite clarity.

I write day
and night not
for strangers
and Mars.
I bear the cross
of critics for you.

show me the
palm of your hand
I will
tell your
fortune in verses
cadences and lines

You spend your
life with Figures
or chanting laws.
The universe is
my book. I
focus through words;
let me take your hand!!

10

The city lies bemused
on a craggy coast
against the Atlantic
where elements fuse.
Purged by waterways
and howling winds
with deception of bell-tones
at the etiolated
unending confluence of patterns;
seated and cross-legged
but only half composed
like green leaves
on dying trees.

A glitter of rock salt
encircled by mountains
she tilts skyward
seaward and skyward
arms stretched outward
in the sun drench
like some shore-washed monster
feeble at the lion's feet
for they are the Lion Mountains;
the Sierra Leone.

Poised at the diastolic
moment of change,

indignant at the deafening
clangour of contrasting possibilities
she sifts realities
at conscience beat;
Amaranthine in the crude
extravagance of her torment
where the sunset wades into the night
and colour on sparkling colour
of tense gaiety
sudden like the change of weather
seeps through her century
of broken passions and near forgotten hope
with the intangible flicker of perfume

But come what may
her every root and hope
lie in the cotton tree
which overlooks the bay.

The people are like the city
The people are the city
come to life
with every subtle change of sundown light
who often fold their hands
over their heads
if not across their breasts.
Their tempers are volcanic and unearthed
but they are rich; so rich in beauty.

There you will see a smile
shimmer like an oasis
and a soul-bound gesture; innocent
pregnant like a heap of roses.
On Sundays they answer the tolling of bells
cling clanging from Goderich to Kent
harnessed in Harris tweed and felt
with lusty voices broad as the Veldt,
the women like plumed chestnut in silver and gold.
But darkness is absence of light
and darkness enhances light.
The people of the city are velvet dark
they blossom at moonfall.

Two seasons alternate
The wet heat and the dry
Ocean breeze desert wind
plough up what they can find;
The people's thoughts are no less protean.

Where energy belongs to nature
God help the human creature
When Homo runs the show
God help Himself.

Their habits and attitudes
ferment between extreme polarities
God has not had an airing
since the anti-slavery laws were passed.

Recreated every Sunday
lavishly entombed on weekdays
because, for ready action
there's no better than the devil.
The after life is all very well
but how about the here and now? by hell!
Daddy Sori, uncle John
Mamma Akosua, Kanimpon
Cockle shell, pigeon droppings
all play their part
when it comes to succeeding.

The city is old and worn
uncoordinated, but full of fun
like her close friend the sun.
She keeps beaming
To seaward leaning
attentive to strange echoes
with a wrinkle and a smile
that imperishable glint in her eye;—
sea drums documenting the future
and every strained moment
which shivers, cracks and blasts in tomorrow.

Every now and then
her indulgent heart is rocked
by new vistas

parcelled in pressurised time
and she moves an inch or two,
nods recognition to me and you.

After the cloud and rain
the sun always shines again.

The city is like any other, but free.
The city is Freetown
From Kroo Bay to Cline Town
Brookfields to Fourah Bay
Free as a summer cloud
and inordinately proud.

11

Atmosphere!
meadows, trees ripe aflame
cattle netted by highways;
masked highways fleeing past
adverts, lights, cables
Noise, squeaking, breaking
grinding heaving, swearing whining
fleeing confusedly into darkness, deep night.

Over there the city
hideously fascinating
reeking of terror, battle cries

blood of mirth decay
wars unconvened.
The battle rages in the heat
cranes witness bedroom scenes
heartbeats stutter, noise
throatcuts, shouts,
blood and the agony of bleeding

Round and round
the cosmic atmosphere of city
lights, hallucinations
doorbells like sirens, telephones
answer the telephone
brake quick; lights changing.
The ground is breaking up;
underground Tubes masturbating
the earth in draughts
an eternal conception.

The jungle is restored
mind the bullet
hold the dagger
turn right turn left
you can't come in here
watch the lights
always the lights
eternal dazzle of stars
head whirling
like the merry-go-round

25

and blood runs thick and deep
O Lady Macbeth
To sleep—only to sleep
to rest and forget
jets exploding in the sky

Infancy!
a moment
one articulated moment of peace
tranquillity;
death

Piece my bones
out of death
imperishable earth
a moment,
a moment
has gone; alas.

12

Penetration is all
heavily nagging
like a mad worm
to a central unity

Reality lies beyond
this comfortable soil
as bird flight
changes with moment

Don't try to reach it
only approach
cautiously with stick
painted half white

Fantasy and imagination
soar like a vice
towards integration
yellow petals in amalgam

Running water
in the park
curls into ice
round a frog's neck

This too is full
of sad meaning
sad significance
and text

Warmth, harlot
of the flesh
brings life together
        enduringly.

13

Clawed green eyed
Feline of night
Palsied breasted
Selling old boot
On wet pavement
In hour-glass baskets.
Coconut bellied
Unyielding Copra
Gland exhausted
Love fatigued
Worm tunnelled sod
Prostituted fruit of Eve
Edging the Park trees
Like dancing caterpillars
In folded leaves
Softened by Social Conscience
Hounded by prudes
Friend of the falling star
Victim of the lonely bed.

14

Consider a snail
you would have
thought its movements
slimy. No, circumspect.
Its towering oblivion
grounded in humility
irritates the idea
of energy. Ten years
to reach some green
morsel on Mars
is nothing to a snail; morally.
Morsel and chlorophyll
will wait embittered
a generation or two
till some waif snail
snaps it up with
less guts; more luck.

Snails fear rapaciousness
prefix for madness,
like lightning ambling
through the sky—where
will it strike or die?
Snails are unerringly
sane and dry.

Let rough winds
carry phantoms into tomorrow.

Winds to hang on
naked desert trees; dateless.
Snails linger obscurely
in the sand, hedges, half shadows
essentially fresh, essentially alive.
Eternally striving, that's all!

15

Open the gates
To East and West
Bring in all
That's good and best

Lay bare the breast
To the unmothered child
Give nipple-comfort
To the doubting guest

Wider still the uninfarcted heart
Large and throbbing as the Universe
Let all come in
With candles burning.

Light the bush-fires
When the stars have fallen
When the moon tires
Of paying homage to heaven

Open the mouth, the eyes and ears
In the new rain
Which washes away the tears
And the sweat stain
Tell those who came
To ravage; of a new world
Of harmony with nature
and strength in goodwill.

16

We have come home
From the bloodless wars
With sunken hearts
Our boots full of pride
From the true massacre of the soul
When we have asked
'What does it cost
To be loved and left alone'

We have come home
Bringing the pledge
Which is written in rainbow colours
Across the sky—for burial
But it is not the time
To lay wreaths
For yesterday's crimes.

Night threatens
Time dissolves;
And there is no acquaintance
With tomorrow.

The gurgling drums
Echo the stars
The forest howls
And between the trees
The dark sun appears.

We have come home
When the dawn falters
Singing songs of other lands
The death march
Violating our ears
Knowing all our love and tears
Determined by the spinning coin.

We have come home
To the green foothills
To drink from the cup
Of warm and mellow bird song
To the hot beaches
Where boats go out to sea
Threshing the ocean's harvest
And the hovering, plunging
Gliding gulls shower kisses on the waves.

We have come home
Where through the lightning-flash

and thundering rain
The famine, the drought
The sodden spirit
Lingers on the road
Supporting the tortured remnants
of the flesh
That spirit which asks no favour
of the world
But to have dignity

17

She came in silken drapes
and naked breasts,
Veiled Artemis; seated
On an eagle's nest
Brandishing the sword
and that forbidden thing
Less clumsy in a dream

She handed me the word
Sealed in cotton wool
Tied in an endless riddle
Love and loveless hate
Poison of the coral snake
Infinitely tender to see
Like Saturn's mystery.

Gentle winged butterfly
with the voiceless cry by day—
Huntress of crippled manhood
Unequal tyrant by night
Visiting the caves of Hysterus
Where the wounded leopard sleeps
In the green light of peace.

Walking in the mist
Among the chambered Monuments
Crowded like icicles
In the patient current
Which feeds by exhaustion,
She smoothes her wrinkles
And prepares for the assault.
Love, lustreless word
A thousand times misused
As often bathed in blood.

Let me wash you
Like the frenzied gold-sifter
Let me lead you
through the dense crowd
over the phallic mound
To the crystal spring
Where I have found
the purest living thing.

18

The first rose of the season
Yellow pink or red
With petals neatly curled
Like the foetal head
Inside an egg
Hinting layer by layer
Under the living dew-drops
At the perfect balance
Of that which is to come
In the full power
Of subdued fragrance.

19

Parachute men say
The first jump
Takes the breath away
Feet in the air disturb
Till you get used to it.

Solid ground
Is not where you left it
As you plunge down
Perhaps head first

As you listen to
Your arteries talking
You learn to sustain hope.

Suddenly you are only
holding an umbrella
In a windy place
As the warm earth
Reaches out to you
Reassures you
The vibrating interim is over.

You try to land
Where green grass yields
And carry your pack
Across the fields

The violent arrival
Puts out the joint
Earth has nowhere to go
You are at the starting point

Jumping across worlds
In condensed time
After the awkward fall
We are always at the starting point

Time was
when I was green
fresh as a meadow
glowing with stars

Summer was universal
endless April
youth unrivalled
Summer to the skies

Barefoot in thorn bush
baked sand
forests, the world
was open to me

My foot trod steadily
in confidence
skin shrieking
with delight

Radiant sunsets
birds, coloured ants
intimacy of flowers
Parrots in a dance

Monkeys tossing
nuts I could not reach
unselfishly in jest
and those who preached

Down foot-charted paths
towards the lake
spread with lotus, lily
and floating skeleton of snake

I would ford across
knee deep pushing my bicycle
beyond the tree of escape
leaf shelter from the sun

In hairy-green valleys
women clad in vegetable
bushes, watering the earth
with sweat and singing

Air heavy with light
had to be cut through
like undergrowth of twigs
and spiders' webs

These I remember
now life has become a system
Yes, and the deep
deep throbbing of the earth

21   *Home Coming*

The present reigned supreme
  Like the shallow floods over the gutters
Over the raw paths where we had been
  The house with the shutters

Too strange the sudden change
  Of the times we buried when we left
The times before we had properly arranged
  The memories that we kept

Our sapless roots have fed
  The wind-swept seedlings of another age
Cultivated weeds have grown where we led
  The virgins to the water's edge.

There at the edge of town
  Just by the burial ground
Stands the house without a shadow
  Lived in by new skeletons

That is all that is left
  To greet us on the home coming
After we have paced the world
  And longed for returning.

22

Messianic conveyances are bogged down
Wrecked; choked with confusion
As summer paths grow obsolete
When the rains come
Here and there camel bones on desert trail
Each once a pillar of two thousand years of life.

Loosen the white sullied collar
Give air, give air for death disturbs the sight
Water! Water! What is that there?
Good God is everything a mirage?

If Christ came down today
Would they recognize His wounded side
And say 'Come home dear wanderer and live with us'?

They would shut Him out
Those who are called by His name
Go away; away
You have nothing more to say
We are deceived; You did not give us
life and vengeance; You are too permanent
too strong; and ignorant of fashion and human want.

Away along the winding road
By the electrocuted mulberry tree
To those in need of loaves and fishes
Across the seas to infant places
Where we have found You a new home

Africans are claiming you for theirs
Ride on, come not again
This time you are contemptuously sold
For even less than gain

We will receive you Lord
For want of a better name
If you can have us as we are
Black skinned, inclined to love
Our human kind.

We will receive you with drums
Dancing and prodigal feasting
Not as an intermediary
To God or truth
On special days and Sundays

We do not befriend
Mortal or spiritual Dictators
But comprehend the glory of your message
so wasted; which rings however dimly in our ears.
Thought before action; others before self
So never letting the confounded world go by
Without adieu.

23 *Wider Excursions*

If I was asked
   How I would face the task
Of camping out in space
   I would reply
With infinite distaste
   That I would rather die.
Because to meddle
   In this confounded puzzle
Would only represent
   My innate discontent.
That if it was my fate
   Men seemed to hate
Then it would be in place
   To offer an estate
On some deserted piece of earth
   Where suited to my girth
And my most earthly temperament
   I would be proud to represent
The non-progressive element.

If I was offered more—
   An offer just as poor,
Perhaps the earth
   As a reward
For traffic up in heaven

I would present
The quite convincing argument
   That far from being competent
The Maker of the instrument
   Should show me how it went.
Thus in the end
   Those minds gone round the bend
Would have all to themselves
   The lunar firmament
And we could laugh
   At what appears daft.
Cows that have jumped the moon.

24   *On History*

The rhythm of the past
Outlives the melody
The jazz and passions burn out
So we don't remember much.

Sparks conflagrate where they fall
And flame with breath of wind
But do not answer questions
Or reiterate conditions.

With luck a moderate incandescence flares
Then suffers exponential decay
This does not however affect the tragedies
Which live till doom's day

When you are picking weeds
It rattles up and straight
Tossing on hypnotic face
Hits you behind the knees

But the muted melody haunts the nights
Arresting distant unsuspecting ears
Still, dreams don't last
And in the heat it is the sweat which counts.

25

One long jump
From the early days
When the face was like a globe
Round, revolving, limitless
Sharp incisive like a probe
And eyes which could see
With the completeness of a globe—geometrically
A soft film of brown hairs
And a language of birds and flowers.

One long jump
From the early days
When wave on wave
Of passion merged
Cutting their losses
Preserving their gains
And beauty tingled the flesh
Like a snake
On the surface of a lake
Yielding her store of comfort
Without deceit
Without fictitious powers of support
And no didactic analyses
To know that milk was sweet.

One long jump
And never another
Never quite the same
Because things get mouldy
in the grave
And milk loses its taste
On the coated tongue.

Bartered birthrite
Like the chaste membrane
Is lost for good
So we can never arrive
At the beginning
To couch in the blue light
Of the primaeval hive,

Except in the dissolution of the flesh;
And early strength never returns
To oppose the grinding artificialities
Or to marvel at the rose.

One long jump
The first and last
and no progression
So take it well!
Looking back upsets
The balanced wheel.
Too tired when we arrive
It is enough
To seek the short cut
To the grave.

26

Yevtushenko disdains
Stalin was a barrier to art
You had to put him in
Like pepper and salt
And then play the part
At least he was a hard nut
To be cracked with a sledge-hammer
Or simple disaster

Here you write as you please
But need a talent without music
Mind without ideas or desires
A bleeding ignorance of form
And language of obscurity
Then you are well mounted
And may even get published
If you don't forget the impotence of sex in words.

You can ruin your art
Trying to please them
Although you know you shouldn't
And that like affluent puppies
They will turn round and bite your fingers.

Look out of the window
The air is free swaying with lilac
Young cheeks are rosy
Malaria is out of the way
But the cold invisible hand
Call him Stalin, Bureaucrat or tramp
Rules the professions, politics, Religion
As well as art, inside and out.

27

Sunset climbs in vain
over the hills
lingers, spills like
blood of the earth
from broken cup
of the earth.
In my heart
I catch drops of it only.

A young moon
punctuates the sky
in vibrio. Shines
segmentally, holds
on to life
watching the sunset die

Cold blister of wind
defines the houses
yonder in braille.
No coughing clouds
only kite-tails
of aeroplanes

Tchaikowsky
in Serenade saw
all this through
snow flakes with
tingling in his brain

Soon the world
sleeps in darkness
mask of infinity.
Lovers on straw fields
will see it again,
cry in cataracts
bridging thighs
in sublime ecstasy.

28

Autumn street
Rushes past my window
In dusty rain—
My calling is vain

Hair-cropped trees
Drowsy in chimney smoke
Drooping shouldered
Chestnut and oak.

Their burnt arms
Reaching together
Crowding to share the sun's
Dislocated embrace

Only a few
Golden tears now
To mourn summer's
Passing death.

Shaking weak wrists
Don't frighten
The dispirited birds
All are waiting.

On slimy pavements
Broken leaves
Recently the pride of Spring
And Summer's canopy

Advance, trembling
In the frenzy of death
Napoleonic Legions
Destined for snow-burial

Behind them
Like shuttered ambulances
Come old women
Stick probing their coffins.

Picking each final step
In which they see
Their death fall
Certain as the leaves

Across the way
Young affectionate thighs
Sweating, unwashed till Spring
Odours of new and decaying years.

I settle in my rolling chair
Hang out my lungs to dry
In tobacco smoke
And wait for another year.

29

Autumn comes
When the veins tingle
And the blood cools
With restless prowling.

Autumn comes
When desire insinuates the flea under the pants.
Desire for the fire
Desire for the warmth
And the freshly made bed
Where joining heads
Two will sow the seed
Through the winter darkness
While the sky flakes
Flutter on the window pane
Hiding the finger marks.

Autumn comes
Before the overtoasted leaves
Before the crisp crunching air
Drops her curtain of mist
And the sun slides
Apologetically out of sight.

Autumn comes
When ants begin to hurry
And sore-throated birds
Think of taking the cure
And our thoughts turn
To the new life
Round winter corner.

30

A tree stares back
With pressing eyes and shakes a branch.

Flowers breathe softly
But smile and almost take your hand.

Dogs will bark
Especially when you meet them in the park.

A ground worm reacts!
It squirms and bleeds and falls in half.

People, cannibals, ghosts, women
Hug, kiss and strangle you
Then leave you like dead wood
To house a toad
Before you can reach them.

Only the wall
And your head
A few feet between
But courage is snug in bed.

31 *On the Death of Winston S. Churchill*

A soul fulfilled
weakens the very fabric of earth
strides out into the broadening dawn
into the serene majesty of death
where epitaphs do not diminish fame
or conflicts rise again.
Trumpeted; trumpeted nobly forth
with chords and billowing hearts
into the cold silence of the grave.
All things were done
all memories kept
though not enough.

Greatness so humbly laid
to rest where leaves in
a fast wind will
stay their vigil; pause
in violent haste to mark the spot,
will guide us yet.
Our hands approach in prayer
our hearts exalt to hear
the Victory of infinite humanity.
Centuries of pomp and ceremonial
will not express so well
as the humblest conscience
breathing, free and sane
the loss our world
will never see again.

32

The panic
of growing older
spreads fluttering wings
from year to year

At twenty
stilled by hope
of gigantic success
time and exploration

At thirty
a sudden throb of
pain. Laboratory tests
have nothing to show

Legs cribbed
in domesticity allow
no sudden leaps
at the moon now

Copybook bisected
with red ink
and failures—
nothing to show the world

Three children perhaps
the world expects
it of you. No
specialist's effort there.

But science gives hope
of twice three score
and ten. Hope
is not a grain of sand.

Inner satisfaction
dwindles in sharp
blades of expectation.
From now on the world has you.

33

Colour of sounds
shapes wasping round
moving concertedly,
the musical sky
pigmented in star notes
tinkling bubbles in cut glass
deep negro, high celtic
sunrise in virile notation
psalmody of sunsets
blue, permanent in blue
excite a future
already dying of neglect.

Wavelengths in counterpoint
tones, spaces
riding endlessly away;
saucy electrons
maddening composure
orderliness of line
unbroken in chaos
discipline of contour.
These are heart beats
of global intensity

Brain conundrum
of shock waves in red,

broken shapes, sound,
palpably sound. Soft
globe squeezes like a balloon
heartbeats in white sound
as pyramids of flame
lisping softly centrally.

On the sea
in stroke of sunlight
water tossing vaporously
alternating forms
breezing in succession.
In a boat
charging on deepest crest
nostrils breathe in frenzy of pain
lashed muscles taut
swing across joints
even the murmur
of factory engines, muted;
marked inches of men's
feet in concrete on the floor
tell of sinking lives
dressed like machines
cocooned in overalls. Point—
Here one lost a finger
There a toe, a job
strike, strike, strike.
Conscience flattens
like stale beer; no matter.

Physical transmutations
carry messages across barriers
to better worlds;
the higher glory of true
essentials.

34

A moment of truth;
beauty, knowing the negative,
clover, mountain top
snow capped, angels in reverse;
obscures the spoken word,
till some cry of pain
not felt reminds you
Wonderful! Magnificent!

Comparison without degree
Summer clad in Winter
to reduce proportion.

How much to gain
in silence. Thought
concreted, emancipated
in feeling not by word.
A rich harvest
like great speeches in Bach.

Evocations intensified
by peace and love.

Words are cumbersome elusive
sophisticated in their demand of skill
Vulgarized by loquacity.

An innermost voice
protests and burrows
with the worm.
Things are not born
of autumn leaves and wind
Visions of purity or saintliness

Things are born of dirt
and ordinariness in the extreme
born out of dirt
and never leaving it
is man's essential nature
always to grovel in it
more debased than the serpent
Mummified in dirt and devastation.

An endless spell
punctuated releases
like champagne corks
herald sublime creations
Man rising out of dirt
with heaviness to reach beyond
as gold is purified by fire

Listen! the agony of the voice
seeking escape whispers
Not only the poet's voice
Philosopher or priest.
Listen! The average human voice
in the domed skyscraper
with every corpuscle in his
veins worth a dollar or more
in the bank his face a mask of success.
Listen to the black cries
in the tenements.
Bread! a hand! a smile!

Both voices one
Speaking of a simple life
in halo of scented flowers
gentle things and sunsets
Spirits, earthly things.

Grave necessity sobers
the voice and will
Great causes, inadequate
rewards conflict; even
with angels behind us.

A tide of passion
rages, revolts,
defies the fatuousness
the injustice, perpetual drama
of Cain and Abel in the field

60

but comes to rest
in silent agony
for loss of power
The controlling fingers
are not God's
but fear triggered
destitute defiance of Man.

To reach God
prayer is not enough
It is necessary to seize Him
compel His presence
demand fulfilment of promise
imprison Him to ferment
and germinate within
He is the sublimate of Men
and the universe

To reach God
Man must transcend
the present moment
Exchange knowledge of self
for that of others
Desisting immediacy
only with intimacy
of universal distress.
To reach God
Man must be worthy
of His image.

35

Fog strangles
With wet hands
And damp intimacy
Squeezing through the skin pores
Like kittens through doors
Filling the passages
Like the brains of drowning men
Oozing through nostrils
So I was told.

Snuggling
Under dark arches
Watching the lighted
Window opposite
Behind the blinds
Shadows mingle

Rancid old women
Cough their haemorrhoids out
Leave it on the table
To show the doctor!
Time to put the light out.
When you wake
The ghost has gone
Leaving the nuptial dew.

36

On a wet September morning
    When vultures hate themselves
On the beach, against the flooded moorage
    Along the rock shelves
Where seagulls lay their eggs
    Half under the cracking waves
With seaweed under my nails
    Where the coastline bends
The sea was not the land's end.

The world under the sea
    The sea under the earth
The sky in the sea
    Were elemental changes of a world
As the true life is death
    Which is the idea inside us
So distinction ends
    The plagued centuries
In a weeping jellyfish
    The pebble that will be a crown
The moon reflected in a starfish.

My amputated feet
    Buried in soft sand
Within the blue shadows
    Were already prehistoric

I tried to leap
   Out of a shark's way
Far from the cutting teeth
   Thundering like a wave
Aimed at my vitals, not my feet.

But they had planted roots
   Among the symbiosing weeds
Which issued from my feet
   Under the caressing current
Where disproportionate time
   Lulled in deep sleep.
I could not move;
   I say I could not move
My vegetable feet;
   But still the tumbling jaws.

Only a silent yell
   Rang through time's corridors
To the farthest end
   Where the amoeba becomes
The fire, water and air;
   Where the primaeval fruit still hangs
So to the other end
   Where planets are but continents
Deep in the future
   That is darker and older
Than the past.

The echo burst inside me
   Like a great harmonic chord
Violins of love and happy voices
   The pagan trumpet blast
Swamping the lamentation of the horn
   Then the heraldic drums
In slow crescendo rising
   Crashed through my senses
Into a new present
   Which is the future.

It was the music
   Floating on salt air
Mixture of ozone and fish, urea
   Boundless in all her forms
Like children's toys
   Which lifted me
Higher than myself
   From the palsied hand of destruction.
       In the vibrations
         Came new awareness
   And care born of feeling
Fear, and the pestilence of thought
Was cradled in a wet pulsating stone.

How then the smell of fish
   The salted lips
Were like violets in a desert waste
   The rancid taste
Her priceless treasury of gems

Hot burning sands
Like the edentulous
Sprouting palms
The sea was the desert
The wet was the dry
Here was there.
All indistinguishable
Like the smell of
Old men's trousers
From the Sunday joint.

37

They dance wildly
threatening violence with
fractured bodies isolated
in moving darkness

The hoarseness snaps
in mid desperation, gropes
flings a message between
eager folds of parched lips

glasses are emptied
drained abandoned
flung like the last
satellite of partners

As morning rises
drowsily abroad they
leave stained carpets, disengage
from scornful embraces

Love making without
transit of love puzzles
disappoints, has to be
repeated like a drug

Their tunnel of desire
could swallow more than flesh
a universe; an immense
spirit gone out of life.

Why work the flesh
to early obsolescence?
Youth burns out its fuel
longing, despising remedy.

Give us a lead
a sign out of strangeness
they cry. A sense of
calamity is not inherited.

My lips too are parched
my heart needs water
it is hard to find
search! search to find.

38

We need the eagerness
of children to listen,
learn, reflect as
well as for milk

Solid self reliance
is worth more than votes
as the voice of a bird
itself creates a meaning

Greatness is needful
and not to be
despised or feared; fear
only the half-leader

The sun disintegrates
in fragments; not
down the middle;
Integration is needful

Flesh and red clay
alike comprehend
the futility of
dissociation

Yet all dissociates
disintegrates like
autumn leaves
people too and love and sunlight.

39 *Lost Friends*

They are imprisoned
In dark suits and air-conditioned offices
Alsatians ready at the door
On the saliva carpeted floor

They spend their nights
In jet airlines—
Would change them in mid-air
To show how much they dare

Drunk from the vertigo
Of never catching their tails
they never seem to know
When not to bite their nails

Their new addiction
Fortifies their livers
They are getting there
While the going's good
They have no time for dreamers.

40

Fading sounds
draw the heart out
pierce indifferent walls
forgotten in the Marathon of life; in sleep
intricate cobwebs of yesterday
floating presently—
golden sunsets, shores
leap from magenta seas
deer angles in flight
deserts dissolve in flood
An increasing dialogue
universally speaking
reaching, growing
arriving, ending, dying
all in a moment's
delicate significance like lovemaking.

Turn the head
look back to catch one note
that isn't there.
Not there; but here
waning in desperate struggle
to bring back strength
we lost foolishly in unwisdom
corrupt conceits.
Measure strength
against the tense distance of longing

against the stars
against the moon kneeling on trees
at the edge of earth.
sighs cascade in silence
feathers on pavements; drift
first one way then another.

Comforts of flesh, self
hang in poisoned row, festooned
impaled on sense
with reckless arrogance.
The mind reflects
the glitter of possessions.

Idleness of shade
wasted eternities
overfed afternoons
run-down dynamos—
illness of lust
moonprobes
cutting like blades
spattered blood of conscience.
Magnolia blossoms
bosoming serpents;
shapes of shadows
dancing, and their shadows.
Aromas, spices, indolent perfumes
caress with maiden hand
exalt impotence of will.

71

Values bought cheaply
of the flesh,
a snore divinely drawn.

Fading sounds
waning strength.
None to stay the lever
of progress, digression.
Up! Up I say
revitalize; by God!
be born again this day.

41

Remember they say the dead
who will rise again
Remember in November
littered bones and ashes of men
in Flanders, Dunkirk, Korea
Burma, Hiroshima
murdered in cold calculation

Remember the scarlet heads
on execution mornings
candid Bavarian mornings
green heaps of human marble
children dying to prove innocence

Remember the aching
silence of despair,
the strangled silence of the moon
in men's hearts.

Remember, yes remember
with trumpets and guns
the helping hand
dripping with blood
Remember the menace is still with us

Remember also the living
two billion weary souls
Let them also have trumpets
for the future has a stronger memory
than the past.

42

Turning the pages of my diary slowly
But rationally under candle light
Halting over entries of bare folly
And the many words I did not write

The sudden shock of scattered references
And 'to be developed' signs
Jotted with unwholesome sentences
And ill-developed rhymes

Pages fastened with candle grease and ink
Remind me I was at least awake
The many evenings when I could not think
But sat enjoying my pulse till daybreak

Turning the chained and fated pages
Was like fumbling with soft life
Melted years mouthed into the ocean
Of pages clouded and wet with tears

But one more page—tomorrow's page
Misty like a reflecting mirror
Showing the shimmering wrinkles of age
And the trenched islands of horror.

The time when sensation goes out of my fingertips
I must distinguish hot and cold by instinct
The time when I must know myself Controller of events
Which have been governed only by the sense

What if I am a recessive mutation
Destined to give way in time
To the surge of biological motion
Which raised the mammal from the reptile?

Then the candle grease and ink
Insomnia and drink
Would be just another link
When I have gone over the brink.

43

The room is ten foot square
ten balding men
mainly from East of Suez
glare like dogs in the mating season—
they're surgeons on parade

Gloom is suppressed
tight as dynamite
where there is no heart left
to offer the sick
twelve years of work and study
only the DOLE to show for it.

John Updike—pale-lipped
fills his expenses form
underlines the paltry sum
4/s or 6/s he's ashamed to ask—
Been in the circus so long
will bite his neighbour on command
He wants to throw a fit and die
when any speak to Updike
about the noble profession—the grovelling profession

Ali in his corner eyes the clock
minutes heavy with bitterness fixed to the wall
accumulate thick drops of years.

Under his breath
he gulps his full-blooded tonic
WHITE MASTERS
WHITE BASTARDS
GRIND YOUR BONES
TO MAKE MY BREAD
a shelf of whores
must know the same humiliation
in the selection game

St John is English serene
and can afford to be
with his squadron of professors
at the rear, hot from Khartoum
TEACH US HOW TO PRAY?
TEACH US HOW TO FIGHT
FOR TRUTH AND FAIR PLAY
St John delights himself
with academic platitudes

Overfed lions won't touch you—SLAVE

The beaming chairman stands
offers you a chair
introduces the members of the Board
Do you sit, stand
or call the whole thing off?
Ankle deep in sweat

Courtesy incarnate strokes his chin—

We have your particulars
but have not read them
Be so good as to tell us
what they do in fact contain!

They want to hear your voice, Perhaps!
I'm looking for a job. . . . Sir . . . s . .s . .s . .

Why do you want this post?

Beggars can't be choosers
Over to Mr X.

What are your plans?
My plans? Survival!
The secretary shakes a scornful head
in all his grey years. . . .
in ANNO NISI DEO
no plans? Come, come!

What are your special interests
in this glorious profession of ours?

Life!

Surely there is an organ
tissue, tract for which
you would lay down your name?

Not even my country.
Over to Mr Y.

You're happy with gastrectomies
Thymectomies, Cardiectomies
Can remove any organ half asleep?

There is disaster in a pause

I want to learn appendicectomies.
A dropped pencil rattles shudders
is silenced by a hand
but silence speaks
with a clatter of cymbals.
TO LEARN?
This is a job—no school for scoundrels
We're not in the middle ages
Automation—self help—self service

Over to Mr Z
who bears the axe over his head
held there by a thread
what . . . I mean . . . what
Sympathy for Mr Z.
Why don't they throw you out?
What are your general interests then?

I am a writer . . . O fatal exchange
six stately heads rocking in their sockets
concern me for their sanity.
One; pre-appointed,
bows in group embarrassment

78

Where do we go from here?
There's never been the like before
He's a newspaper spy

Salt's bad for earthworms
straight talk for surgeons
but better not to wait or pray
another train to catch
the masochistic ritual—
some twenty miles—is under way.

44

Steady reacquaintance will keep alive
the vast consciousness of the past
which struggles for a place with us now.
Connecting future to past as air to earth
Lest all contact be deprived.

Though maimed by time it carries a voice of steel
and channels like hardened arteries
Their pulsations detectable by electronic machines.

They can absorb a part of this despair
Of flesh and mind; corrosion of overripe confidence
they know which emptied the blood of history
Into our fenestrated tuft of vessels
Spilling not a few drops.

But it is not conceit or lack of interest
Which hermetically seals our ways
It is the swift passing of molecular time
Diffracted by our fact encrusted lives
Which mollifies the contact.

The Grid survives in sustentacular
Protuberance with stores of current
To light our way at the turning of a screw.

45

In the beginning
one voice
one cry
one promise
out of the dark wilderness
One struggle
for paged history
Indivisible
in the clasped visor
of common purpose.
Rivers flamed with blood
echoed low hanging clouds
the yearning crowds
their rampant flow of tears.

The dark continent
awoke from sleep
cocked up its ears
in the swelter of a dream
and heard the devil speak.
Take!
take and eat
Know yourselves—
Gods of the central East
the bone
in the white man's gullet,
assume the throne.

We heard the politicians
Saviours of a nation
of the race.
We saw
bitterness of our hearts
in their eyes
their days of sorrow
years of prison.
We heard
voices hoarse with shouting,
saw faces rubbed in the mud
attempting to smile.
Azikiwe, Nkrumah
Kenyatta, Nyerere, Kaunda
round the flinted Pork-chop
to Jawara.

Each a giant in his place.
We listened, wept, cheered
thought we understood each face.
They were glorious days
shouting and fervour
the tension of a bent reed.

We heard
'Down with Imperialists'
'Down with Capitalists'
about dogmas of the East
corruption from the West.
We heard
about Socialism
the equal sharing of goods
freedom, the new Africa
the African personality
then the word
which crazed and touched the sky
Unity.
Unity after freedom was the cry.
Unity across the offal of Imperialism
Unity after Uhuru.

As innocents we believed
with love in our hearts
        we believed
with trust of zealous love
        we believed.

Did not think then
the ravings of hot heads
or the promises of foxes
rolled up our sleeves
avenged the slavery of the past.

Each man in his heart
with a wish, a vote
with brawn and elbow grease
played his part.
The peasant in the field
the clerk
the labourer with his sack
bowed heads to the tool
            in hand
raised voices to the sky
Freedom, unity, prosperity
We shall abolish
the Tse Tse fly.

Meanwhile
the Politicians came and went
Meteors about the sky—
it was necessary to seek loans
to beg in style
it will cost each of you
            a meal a day.
The taxes rose
The Common income fell
the death rate stayed alive.

But excuse me, sir;
We're free.
Why do we have to beg?
Industrial development
Dams, factories, the lot—
change the face of the Continent.
'I see
But my children—
beg pardon Sir,
will they go to school?'
Later!
'Will they have food to eat
and clothes to wear?'
Later I tell you!
'Beg pardon Sir;
a house like yours?'
Put this man in jail.

Days have been quick in passing
Contracts long drawn out
Where are the schools, hospitals, jobs
the sharing out of goods?
As usual
those white men tricked us
left the platter clean
only enough for Ministers and Queens.
As for unity
go have your head examined
What do you want it for?

We have enough to eat and drink
Have just negotiated aid
those people over there across the Continent
Have problems hot as hell—
Do you want to tote the
black man's burden?
Besides we have little in common
(except black skins) with them.
Let each look to himself—
that's what the white man taught us,
                              be content.

We earned our Independence
Let South Africans do the same.
The brotherhood of race,
of Man's a myth
only your social status counts.
We have money, power . . .
not as much as we would like
a lauding thriving corrupted middle class
Unity my arse.

They promised once
led us to believe
it was our only hope.
We starved as slaves, colonials
then home-made slaves again.
we'd starve a little more
for Unity.

I'll tell you what!
We'll have an OAU
to keep them guessing
don't for a moment
think it'll work
but just for luck
Man! stop looking at the clock.

A conference.
Everything must start with conferences.
A conference was convened
in a suitable climate
to demonstrate to all the world
African solidarity and regiment
some power to be reckoned with.

What happened?
It was a humid day
tempers quite near the boil
One rose to speak
the murmuring spread—
I am the leader of all Africa

I will be heard in silence
Then tempers flared
first to the heights of sarcasm
How can you lead
what does not yet exist?
Set your own house in order
African Unity means democracy.

It was a humid day
and foul winds blew
the conference broke in two;
down East and West
with many splintered in.

When next we meet
we'll put up a better show.
The jackals got their bone
and laughed, and laughed, and laughed.

The Congo crises came and went
the OAU gesticulated, jeered, fell apart.

The Chinese then stepped in
We're brothers
of different mothers
bonded against the common foe
but so to speak
your elder brothers
depend on us
and we shall lead you by the nose.
They came in friendship
established embassies
we stretched out a hand
they paid a modest dowry.
Then silently at first
Louder they showed their pride
admonished leaders they disliked
Interfered with conferences

generally pushed folk around.
What's happening?
First white then black
now yellow Imperialism.
We're Communists brothers
to help you build Black Socialism.
Only you must kick out the Russians.
All this went on
The vultures picking here and there
Our leaders building cobwebs in the sky
We were used to arrogance
to nonentities but had yet
to see the supreme exponent of both.
A name
emerged
as common as the sand
Smith.
What Smith?
Ian Smith.
Ridiculous.
Yes he's defied the odds
and threatened UDI
Ian Smith won't dare
our black brothers will resist
the OAU will swallow up
Rhodesia like this
and smack her lips.
If not, the British have
too much at stake.

These the black Leaders
each in his cell refusing
to coordinate their policies.

True the OAU threatened
made gestures at the UNO.
like some nocturnal creature
retired at noon-day.
All watched
with heads bowed down with shame
another challenge to Britain and the OAU
but neither took the blame.
Smith went to London
London went to Smith

In the end
Smith slipped through the net.

There is hunger and sickness
                    in the land
I say there is a cauldron burning
                    on that plain
red earth, red vengeance
                    all aflame
          must it be born in vain?
I carry a ball of fire
                    on my head
and cannot put it down
I pray for rain, for vital floods
                    to come again.

The oceans lick my toes
                    rush downhill with time
I burn in my heart,
in that desolate plain
raped, plundered, decimated.
There are ghosts like wailings
                    in empty spaces
waves of acrid flesh
                    passionless wind.
cracks in my bones are gummed together
like the units of that place
Save it; save the wreck
your lives a pledge
Unity come back
embrace it
hold it
as in the beginning
In the end
One voice
One people
out of the dark struggle.

46

A sabre shark
lifts and plunges
cutting the emerald
sea like firewood
a spray of steam
angles the lightning track
towards the fossil
of the sea bed.
An immense danger
ripples away
stabs centrally
by flashes and shadows
with a clean intention
cast in a single grim desire.
My eye loses track
in a wink
The monster tosses and gulps
existence is in its belly
Truth is naked
to be slashed at cleanly
shedding ceremonial robes
of undesirable thoughts
emotions, words
complexes. Diving pneumatically
not with acolytes and candles,
cleaned sharply to the bone
like a skilled executioner.

47

Forgotten song
Buried under the egg heap
Where the voice broke
Before it learned to speak
Before the years
Of bird-footed sleep
Scattered the nerves
And honey-soaked memory
Seeped from
The needled brain

I know you are untamed

When the harsh laughter dies
And the long night
Fills the lung
With fresh air
When the tired mind
Knows feeble silence
I separate the yolk
Made delicate with years
Lying voiceless
With my forgotten song.

48 *On Exploding the Chinese Bomb*

Convulsions of horror
undermine a day of explosions
six hundred million catastrophes
spearing the throbbing heart of life
by one idea..
A bomb, a fissioned nucleus
lights the Eastern sky with horror!
Cloud of debasement
shuddering hugely like a sun
lost in the dust of no direction
worms mutilate and corrupt
in unspeakable darkness of deep night
Prestige and chaos of world vandalism
ignites primitive fears. Life and death
of soul fries in the balance.
I have seen the sword dancer
loose contact with himself
go mad in action
in violation of himself
without component of restraint.
Sacrifice the world to nothingness
blood from the depths of lunacy.
Men of simple hearts tremble
recall Napoleon's vision,
and wish him here.
We know the horror
from those who gave it birth

We are but pygmies
innocent and sweet of breath;
Mothers of the West
transmitted the vile disease
Let them chew their profane
breasts and weep, weep
For children they have borne
and suckled out of hate
weep from the womb;
one devastating seed
sown in the wilderness of hate
poisoning the flesh of earth,
weep that night will never sleep
in the wisdom of peace

Black eyes in separate worlds
observe the agony
hands clasped, knife edges
scissored at their throats.
The agony of despair
will come after the hand shaking,
kissing, the oases of aid
when clouds rise in the Eastern sky
to shut out the sun.
Black saints will not save them then
nor anger or subservience.
Events mirror a clock face
the hands move on till
all is wound out.

The last message of goodwill
came from the East
from lowly Bethlehem
with straw and asses feet
Let the West show
one act of greatness
A magnanimity supremely
selflessly given.

49

Railway stations
Stony provincial
rustle like autumn
Stop, beginning link   Fleeting spirits
                          rush through
                          from yesterday
                          and another season

Neither early
nor late
continuation
between time and place   Shadows appear
                          from nowhere
                          heavily aimless
                          sumptuously intense shadows

something moves
inside and out

wheels chanting
in red smoke   There are cats
               of course pleasure
               seeking; evidently
               also rats and brats.

Elbowing carriages
going mistakenly
where? shuffle
to keep going   A church mounted
               opposite warms with
               glass images in gold
               the sun drops limp at my feet

Pressure to keep
going devours
the will to survive, to halt
with a temperature   carriages, images
                     angles confluent
                     unutterably in silent statement.

Whistle of wind
catch the wind
seize it, put it in chains
Expressly stated.   Next stop
                  Inverness
                  or where
                  the mind rests

Excitement, the unknown
revolving madly
like drums, drums
and high pitched dancers.

96

50

Where are the banners now
Which once we carried high
When we led the people
To the shrine of freedom
Banners stained for all time
Like this chocolate skin
With blood from the lacerated womb

The slogans we threw about like fireworks
Which disfigured the alien face
Are reflected from outer space
And have landed like Meteorites
In the crowded squares
The children are cut in pieces
And their cries will still be heard tomorrow

Why are the flags still at half-mast?
Have they forgotten it was to mark
The death of our recent history
Is there death in the land
That the flags do not fly high
And free for all to see?
Has the fertile wind altered
That the flags hang limp and still
In a sky of unchanging blue.

Who will climb into the broad plains
Where they can see the tattered crowd
Women beating their heads in sorrow
Because their men are made impotent with guilt.

Who will look down from the Eagle's crater
Secured inside the solid rock
And bring us the Tablets yet again
On which the promises and the Law stand out in gold.

51

The seagulls return
After the flood
To find their nests gone

Cry after piercing cry
Fills the air
As they fly high

Because they have seen
Calamity that might have been
They beat their wings
Like Muslims in prayer

The vulture moans—
Tomorrow he will build a nest
But soon forgets

98

The sun is enthroned;
Wrapping the leaves in gold
She gives new life to the old

The Lily smiles
Spreading her moistened lips to say
How good to be alive today.

52

Stand up for yourselves
And us.
Tell us what you like
Not what we ought
Before the toad-bellies
Belch us out
And leaves us there to rot.

Gentle, uninformed,
Work-a-day public
Undisguise yourself
And come to meetings
Where culture is discussed
In language from the moon
By tired cross-lined exchange
Of professionals.

Men who have fed too long
And too quickly
On green apples
Develop an aversion for fruit
And find more comfort
In the lavatory,
Reading their own books.

Though they may tell you
What to read
Do not hesitate to plead
For what you need.
It may not bring them gold
But Hell! Far too much is
Bought and sold.

53

After they put down their overalls
And turn off the lathes
They do not return to the women
After they have bathed
Instead, with Hyena's thirst
They run to the open-air bar
To swallow the hook of imported liquor
As they sit reckless across the log
Hypnotised by the bees.

They belch the arrogance of doubt
As they lie in refined stupor
Waiting for the sharp sun
To show them the way out.
Less sure than when they took the potion
They lumber back to the clever tools
They do not love and do not understand
Hoping the sun's anger would cool
So they can carry their dark glasses in their hand.

54

Every time they shut the gates
And hang up notices
On steel plates
That love-making is forbidden
After eight
Someone pulls down the place

Every time the conceited few
Decide they know best
And ought to set the pace
The lazy crowd makes haste
To put them in their place

Confused restrictions everywhere
Some tell you what to wear
Others how to do your hair
They even teach you how to die
And what to do as soon as you get there.

55

I shall return
When daylight saunters on
When evening shadows the berry
And fiery night the sun.
I shall return
With unslippered feet
When I have done with spear and shield
And a lion's tongue
To show I have destroyed the beast.

But first I must
Burn away the fever
And dissolve the nerves
While promise hangs
In the clear air
And my young sinews
Flex the hand
While the pomegranate glows
On the parched hillside
And the hurricane of passion slows.

O to dissolve
On the chemist's tripod
Into the wholesome
Phantasmagoria of love—
To sublimate in truest crystal
Into the fluorescent harmony
Before the retina perish,
And the worms flourish.

To be perfused into
The noble greatness of life
To release my inner power
Against false barriers and strife
Then to unite the energies
Of the sexual bower
Before I knock on the locked
Gates of hell.